Original title:
Vivid Twists Above the Witch Yarn

Copyright © 2025 Swan Charm

Author: Lan Donne
ISBN HARDBACK: 978-1-80563-472-0
ISBN PAPERBACK: 978-1-80564-993-9

Whimsy Sown in Celestial Yarn

In a garden where starlight plays,
The moonlight dances, soft and bright,
Petals whisper of forgotten days,
As magic weaves through the night.

Dreams drift softly on midnight air,
Each twinkling spark a tale to share,
With laughter hiding in shadows near,
And hope ignites in every prayer.

Hidden secrets in the breeze,
Like fairies fluttering, wild and free,
Mirthful giggles weaving glee,
Painting worlds only few can see.

Glimmers of joy in every thread,
A tapestry spun with care and love,
Where every heart has gently bled,
In harmony with stars above.

Oh, the stories that colors hold,
In twilight's blush, the heart grows bold,
With every stitch, a legend told,
Crafted from wishes, bright as gold.

The Illusion of Patterns in the Sky

In the vastness above our gaze,
Constellations weave a splendid tale,
A dance of light in celestial haze,
As dreams unfurl on a silver trail.

Shapes emerge from the cosmic sea,
Whispering secrets, mysterious and sly,
Yet fleeting like shadows, they seem to be,
Sparkling wonders across the sky.

Patterns shift, like thoughts in flight,
Illusions drawn in midnight's art,
Every twinkling dot ignites the night,
As starlit stories touch the heart.

We search for meaning, our eyes aligned,
In cosmic designs both grand and strange,
Yet find that sometimes, the stars unwind,
Leaving us lost in a boundless range.

So let us dream and not despair,
For each night paints for us anew,
The patterns we chase on a breath of air,
Are fleeting wonders, all too true.

Whispers of Magic Woven in Twilight

As twilight wraps the world in gold,
Whispers of magic stir the air,
With secrets of the night foretold,
And dreams undone, laid bare.

Shadows stretch beneath the trees,
Where enchanted spirits wander free,
With laughter rippling on the breeze,
And echoes of a wild decree.

In the quiet hush of dusk's embrace,
The stars awaken, one by one,
Inviting us to join the chase,
For wonders waiting to be spun.

Beneath the arch of twilight's dome,
Mysteries bloom in softest shades,
Inviting hearts to roam and roam,
And weave through night, where magic fades.

So listen close, when shadows gleam,
For every whisper holds a key,
To unearth the depths of every dream,
And dance with echoes of the sea.

Threads of Fate Under Starry Skies

Under the vast and shimmering night,
Where threads of fate in silence loom,
Each star a promise, pure and bright,
We weave our wishes through the gloom.

Tangled paths entwined we tread,
With unseen hands that guide our way,
In the tapestry of life, we're led,
By fate's own hand, come what may.

As comets flash and shooting stars,
Cross the canvas of the sky,
We glimpse the truth in cosmic bars,
And ponder truths that flutter by.

In these moments, hearts ignite,
As destinies dance in the cosmic flow,
Threads of twinkles pull us tight,
In the night's embrace, we come to know.

For every wish we dare to make,
In starlit dreams, we find our place,
Through thread of fate, we will awake,
And dance through night, with hope's sweet grace.

Shadows Playing Among the Fibers

In twilight's grasp, the shadows dance,
Among the threads of fate's advance.
They weave a tale both dark and bright,
In fabric realms, of day and night.

Each fiber holds a secret sway,
A whispered truth that fades away.
In corners dim, they twine and spin,
As dreams take shape and softly begin.

Beneath the loom, the echoes hum,
Of stories trapped, yet yet to come.
With every pull, the shadows flirt,
In hidden seams where wishes skirt.

Illusions twirl, a spectral play,
In patterned threads, where visions lay.
A dance of light, a prance of dark,
In woven worlds, they leave their mark.

So craft with care, each stitch and loop,
For magic brews in this fine group.
In shadows' grip, the fibers sigh,
As tales unfold and dreams can fly.

Shimmering Hues of the Witching Hour

As night descends, the air grows thick,
With shimmering hues, both bright and slick.
The whispering stars begin to gleam,
A tapestry spun from the realm of dreams.

In every shade, a story glows,
Of wandering souls and lost echoes.
The moonlight bathes the world in grace,
In witching hour's enchanted space.

Silken threads of twilight dance,
In every glance, a fleeting chance.
With brushes dipped in cosmic flow,
The night reveals what we can't know.

In gardens lush where shadows blend,
The colors shift, and whispers send.
A world unseen, yet close at hand,
In shades of magic, bold and grand.

So linger long, as dreams ignite,
In shimmering hues, the heart takes flight.
For in this time, the veil is thin,
Allow the wonders to seep in.

The Yarn of Wonder and Whimsy

In a cozy nook, the yarn lies curled,
A ball of wonder in a secret world.
With colors bright and threads of gold,
It spins a tale just waiting to be told.

A soft embrace, a gentle tug,
In every loop, a longing hug.
From crafty hands, the magic flows,
In playful patterns, the heart bestows.

Each stitch a spark of joy and cheer,
In wondrous realms where dreams appear.
The yarn entwines, no plan unspun,
In whimsical dances, we find our fun.

With needles clicking, hearts align,
As wonder blooms from every line.
A tapestry of laughter and tears,
In woven dreams throughout the years.

So gather round and spin with glee,
In our yarn of whimsy, wild and free.
For every thread that leaves our hands,
Unfolds the magic of countless lands.

Dreams Entangled in Silken Whispers

In silk's embrace, the dreams reside,
Entangled deep where secrets hide.
With every sigh, a whisper grows,
In tender tones, the magic flows.

Beneath the stars, their voices weave,
A soft refrain, that none perceive.
In shadows cast by moonlight's gleam,
The dreams awaken, entwined in dream.

As morning breaks, the silken threads,
Embrace the light where vision treads.
In fluttered hopes and gentle sighs,
The whispers guide where yearning lies.

So hold them close, these fragile dreams,
In silken whispers, the heart redeems.
For in their depth, the magic grows,
A soft ballet 'neath willow bows.

With every pulse, in quiet night,
The dreams entwined inspire flight.
In silken hush, they dare to soar,
Through whispered tales forevermore.

Storms and Stitches of Atmosphere

In shadows where the thunder grumbles,
The clouds weave tales in bustling evenings.
Each droplet writes a story,
Of battles fought in whispered breezes.

The winds howl like lost spirits,
Carrying secrets from afar.
Lightning paints the sky with magic,
Unraveling mystery in a dance.

Threads of rain connect the earth,
Binding dreams in a wet embrace.
Nature's loom, forever stitching,
With every gust, a new refrain.

The night holds its breath in silence,
Eyes glittering like scattered stars.
But storms soon pass, and calm will follow,
Stitches left in the quiet dusk.

The Loom of Dreams and Nightfall

In a world where shadows linger,
Dreams are spun like silver threads.
Each night, a space for wonder,
Where whispers waltz through azure skies.

Moonlight weaves a tapestry,
Of stories told in hushed tones.
Stars provide the twinkling stitches,
Sewing fables from the heart.

Time unfolds like a delicate shawl,
Embracing dreams, both big and small.
With every sigh, night falls deeper,
Cradling hopes in its velvet arms.

A loom of secrets, bright and pale,
In twilight's hold, where spirits sail.
The dawn will come with gentle fingers,
But now, we dwell in night's embrace.

Colorful Chronicles of the West Wind

The West Wind carries tales anew,
Of fields ablaze with golden hues.
Flowers dance in cheerful laughter,
Painting dreams with fragrant bursts.

Drifting softly through the valleys,
It whispers secrets of the past.
Each breeze a brushstroke, vibrant,
Creating worlds that ever last.

From sunlit shores to shadowed hills,
The colors blend in playful spins.
Every petal tells a story,
Of joy, of sorrow, of sweet chimes.

The canvas of the skies ignites,
With hues of dusk and dawn's delight.
Yet in this tapestry of wonder,
The West Wind reigns, both fierce and kind.

Nighttime Whirls of Wish and Wonder

In velvet cloaks, the stars emerge,
Spinning whirls of wishful light.
The moon hums softly to the night,
Crafting magic in twilight's peace.

Whispers cling to every breeze,
As dreams take flight on silver wings.
A hush cascades over the world,
Where wishes bloom like timid flowers.

Glowing orbs of hope and desires,
Scatter across the cosmic sea.
Each heart beats with unspoken dreams,
In this realm of endless wonder.

The night embraces all with grace,
Unraveling secrets of the stars.
In these whirls, we find our paths,
Guided by the light within.

Whispers of Enchanted Threads

In a realm where shadows play,
Threads of silver weave their say.
Whispers dance through air so light,
Enchanting hearts with hidden might.

Wistful dreams upon the loom,
Stitching hope, dispelling gloom.
Every fiber tells a tale,
Of magic's touch, of love's frail veil.

Through twilight's soft and gentle kiss,
We find the threads we dare not miss.
They bind our fates, both near and far,
Woven deep like a guiding star.

In the night, as secrets blend,
Each woven stitch, a sacred mend.
With every knot, a wish is spun,
Under the watch of moon and sun.

So listen close to whispers clear,
Of enchanted threads that draw us near.
For in their weave, our souls will soar,
In wondrous tales forevermore.

Dancing Shadows on the Loom

In the stillness of the night,
Shadows dance in soft moonlight.
On the loom, they twist and twine,
Crafting dreams from tales divine.

Every step, a soft refrain,
Echoes of a long-lost pain.
Threads entwined with secrets old,
In the weaving, stories told.

As they move, the fabric sways,
Carrying whispers of olden days.
Each shadow bends, each step profound,
In their dance, magic is found.

With nimble ease, they navigate,
Through threads of fate, we hesitate.
In that motion, hope unglues,
Reviving dreams we dare to choose.

So let the shadows take their flight,
Throughout the vast expanse of night.
For in their dance, we find a way,
To weave our dawn from yesterday.

Tales Spun in Midnight's Glow

In twilight's embrace, stories abide,
Spun with care on fate's dark tide.
Each tale glowing with ancient lore,
Tales spun tight, forevermore.

Beneath the stars, they gently gleam,
Whispers weaving through every dream.
Midnight's touch, a silken thread,
Binding the living with the dead.

As shadows flicker, plots unwind,
In every twist, a truth we find.
With every stitch, our fears take flight,
In the glow of the deep, cool night.

Magic lingers in the air,
Breathing life into tales we share.
Under moon's watchful, knowing gaze,
We trace the paths of mystic ways.

So gather 'round, let stories flow,
In every line, a spark will grow.
For in this weave, our souls ignite,
In the tapestry of love and light.

Threads of Moonlight and Magic

In the hush of the evening dark,
Moonlight threads a glowing arc.
Casting visions upon the ground,
Where old secrets can be found.

Each strand shimmers with a spell,
Tales of wonder, deep to tell.
Magic flows through each soft line,
Speaking softly, divine design.

As wishes dance in the cool night air,
We weave our hopes with tender care.
Fingers brush against the seams,
Where the fabric holds our dreams.

In this light, all fears erase,
Resilience found in every place.
So let us weave, let us create,
A wondrous fate that does await.

With threads of moonlight, we embark,
Each stitch ignites a tiny spark.
For in this magic, we entwine,
Our stories bold, forever shine.

Spirals of Enchantment in the Breeze

Whispers dance through emerald leaves,
A song of magic softly weaves.
Each flicker holds a tale untold,
Of dreams unfolding, brave and bold.

In shadows cast by twilight's glow,
The secrets of the wild do flow.
With every breath, the crisp air sings,
Of splendid worlds and wondrous things.

A melody on soft winds blares,
As starlight sparkles, love declares.
The spirals twirl, both fierce and light,
Enchantment weaves through day and night.

Beneath the arching, silver skies,
The moonlit charm, our spirits rise.
Together lost in spinning grace,
In every corner, magic's trace.

With every note, the heart takes flight,
In the embrace of the gentle night.
A world reborn, with every breath,
Spirals of enchantment, life and death.

Looming Spirits of the Forest

In shadows deep where whispers hide,
Looming spirits roam with pride.
Their forms are cloaked in ancient lore,
Guardians of the forest floor.

Through tangled roots and timeless trees,
They carry tales upon the breeze.
Echoes soft of ages past,
In every glance, memories cast.

With glimmers bright, they softly tread,
Through twilight paths where others dread.
In hollow glades their laughter weaves,
A tapestry that never leaves.

If you should hear the night's refrain,
Know that woods are not in vain.
Spirits loom, both wise and kind,
In every rustle, magic blind.

So lift your heart to whispers old,
In stories new, let dreams unfold.
For 'neath the stars and trees profound,
Looming spirits dance around.

Serpentines in a Luminous Maze

Winding paths of glowing light,
Serpentines sway, a wondrous sight.
Each turn a secret, bright allure,
In the heart of night, so pure.

Through labyrinths of emerald glow,
A flickering dance, the shadows flow.
With every twist, the magic hums,
Awakening dreams where stillness drums.

Dancing softly, the moonlight streams,
Carving out a place for dreams.
As whispers rise in soft embrace,
Serpentines lead to a hidden space.

In the depths where silence sings,
And every step, a feathery fling,
The maze unfolds its tender flight,
Serpentines weaved in silken night.

A journey woven with fate's own hands,
In luminous paths, the spirit stands.
Through every corner, wonder stays,
Serpentines twirl in radiant rays.

Echoes of Magic on the Wind

Listen close, oh gentle heart,
Echoes whisper, never part.
Through the fields where shadows play,
Magic lingers, night and day.

Each gust a tale, both old and wise,
Floating softly through the skies.
With every breath, the magic stirs,
In timeless dance, the spirit whirs.

From mountain peaks to valleys deep,
The ancient secrets softly creep.
In echoes sweet, the stories blend,
A promise kept, while darkness bends.

Awakened dreams in every note,
On the wind, the magic floats.
A tapestry of sound divine,
Echoes call across the brine.

So heed the song, let it begin,
In every gust, the heart shall spin.
For echoes carry tales anew,
Of magic's grace, both bright and true.

Chromatic Secrets of the Night's Fabric

In twilight's soft embrace, colors seep,
Threads of magic wane, quietly deep.
Stars whisper secrets in hues so bright,
A tapestry woven from shadows of night.

With each gentle breeze, the whispers roam,
Calling the dreamers to weave their own home.
Cornflower and ruby, on silken strands,
Dance in the hands of enchanted lands.

Moonlight drips gold on the edge of despair,
Painting illusions in the cool night air.
Caught in the shimmer of every weave,
Are hopes that we dare not ever believe.

In silence, the colors begin to blend,
Under the watch of the lantern's bend.
Mysteries linger in dusk's warm quilt,
Where shadows and colors are tenderly built.

Guardians of the Weaving Moon

Beneath the moon's watchful, silver gleam,
The guardians gather, as if in a dream.
With nimble fingers, they shape and mend,
The fabric of wishes that night can lend.

Each stitch holds a tale of love and woe,
Patterns spun from the heart's gentle glow.
In the still of night, they toil and weave,
For every lost soul that dares to believe.

They sing to the stars, their voices so sweet,
Melodies woven in rhythmic beat.
From echoes of laughter, to cries of despair,
They stitch every promise, each longing prayer.

In the depths of the night, their magic is spun,
Under the gaze of the watching sun.
When dawn breaks anew with its golden light,
The guardians fade until the next night.

Kaleidoscope of Secrets and Sorcery

In a kaleidoscope spun of shadow and light,
Secrets unmask in the stillness of night.
Whirls of enchantment twirl and take flight,
A dance of the mystics, both silent and bright.

Patterns unfold in the whispers of dreams,
Crafting a world where nothing is as it seems.
Each color a truth, each shade a deceit,
In this realm of wonder, where fate and joy meet.

Through lenses of starlight, the visions flow,
Magic in motion, a soft, velvet glow.
Twists and turns in this enchanted array,
Guide wandering spirits who lose their way.

With threads of the cosmos, the fabric's spun,
An intricate tale that begins with the sun.
In the kaleidoscope's heart, our secrets take hold,
Woven in whispers, both ancient and bold.

Midnight Stitches of the Ethereal

In midnight's embrace, where shadows reside,
The ethereal stitchers have nothing to hide.
With needles of starlight, they weave in the dark,
Creating a symphony, a luminescent spark.

Each stitch tells a story, a moment in time,
Woven together, a mystical rhyme.
As moonbeams cascade on the fabric so fine,
The secrets of night in the fabric entwine.

Delicate whispers spin in the air,
As spirits of twilight dance everywhere.
Crafting the echoes of laughter and tears,
Stitching the fabric of dreams and of fears.

In the heart of the night, the ethereal weave,
Holds whispers of magic for those who believe.
As dawn gently breaks, they retreat from the sight,
Leaving behind the soft warmth of night.

Phantoms in the Velvet Weave

In twilight's grasp, the shadows grow,
Whispers weave through threads of woe.
Phantoms dance in silken light,
Their tales entwined, in endless night.

A tapestry of dreams undone,
Each stitch recalls what was once fun.
Fingers trace the patterns lost,
In velvet folds, they bear the cost.

The mirrors glint, a gaze so deep,
In nightly haunt, the phantoms creep.
With laughter soft, they call your name,
A haunting tune, a ghostly game.

From time to time, a thread pulls tight,
Binding hearts in the cold moonlight.
They weave their stories, old and new,
In velvet shadows, the phantoms strew.

Yet when dawn breaks, and colors shine,
The echoes fade, the weavings twine.
In memory's depth, the phantoms stay,
In velvet weave, they find their way.

The Sorceress' Clever Knots

In a quiet glen, where secrets dwell,
A sorceress weaves her magic spell.
With nimble fingers, she ties each strand,
Binding fate with a deft hand.

Her knots hold whispers of ages past,
Stories of love, of shadows cast.
Each twist reveals a hidden lore,
A tale of wonder forevermore.

The moonlight glints on her sacred thread,
Illuminating paths where few have tread.
With every pull, the world aligns,
As destiny dances in tangled lines.

The sorceress sings to the creaking trees,
While secrets swirl on a playful breeze.
Her clever knots are fate's embrace,
A tapestry spun in time and space.

And as dawn breaks, she whispers low,
"Remember the ties that gently flow.
For every knot, a journey starts,
In the fabric of dreams, we play our parts."

Enigma of the Starlit Loom

Beneath the night, a loom does glow,
With fibers fine, where stardust flows.
Each thread a mystery, a cosmic tale,
In the quiet hum, where spirits sail.

The weaver stands in silence deep,
With dreams enshrined, in shadows steep.
Her fingers dance like softest breeze,
Creating wonders with graceful ease.

An enigma spun from light and dark,
In every weave, a hidden spark.
Galaxies whisper in rhythmic tune,
As the yarn unwinds beneath the moon.

The starlit loom, a tapestry grand,
Holds the echoes of a distant land.
With colors bright, it tells the lore,
Of things unseen, and paths ignored.

And when the dawn beckons the night,
The threads will blend into morning light.
With every piece, the cosmos shifts,
In the loom of dreams, the mystery lifts.

Whispered Secrets in the Fabric

In every fold lies a secret kept,
A tapestry where memories slept.
Whispers linger in the silken threads,
Echoes of laughter, tears unshed.

Each stitch a promise, a life unfurled,
In vibrant hues, a hidden world.
The fabric breathes with stories untold,
Of love, of loss, of dreams bold.

Through time's gentle hands, the fabric flows,
Gathering all that the heart knows.
With every swish, a sigh escapes,
A melody formed, in timeless shapes.

Listen closely, and you might hear,
The whispers soft, a voice so dear.
In every seam, a moment's grace,
In the fabric's heart, a sacred space.

As dusk descends and shadows play,
The whispers dance and drift away.
Yet in each thread, and every seam,
The fabric holds our secret dream.

Enchanted Stitches in Cosmic Blue

In twilight's weave, the stars align,
Threads of magic, so divine.
They twinkle softly, weave their art,
A tapestry that calls the heart.

Each stitch a whisper, night unfurls,
Whispers of dreams from distant worlds.
With needles made of silver light,
They sew the shadows into night.

In cosmos bright, the wonders sing,
A dance of fate, a hidden spring.
With every twirl, new paths appear,
A cosmic quilt that draws us near.

Glimmers of hope in every seam,
We navigate through starlit dreams.
The fabric glows with ancient lore,
Infinite skies forevermore.

As dawn's first rays begin to chase,
The stitches hold, time can't erase.
A tale of magic in the blue,
In every thread, a wish comes true.

The Loom of Celestial Dreams

Beneath the moon, the loom does spin,
A tapestry where dreams begin.
With threads of hope and whispers sweet,
It weaves the stars beneath our feet.

Each night, it calls to hearts so bold,
A story whispered, yet untold.
In colors bright, the cosmos gleams,
A swirling dance of vivid dreams.

The weaver's touch, both soft and wise,
Creates a world that mesmerizes.
With every stroke, a life awakes,
In starlit realms, the magic shakes.

A flicker here, a shimmer there,
The loom sparks joy into the air.
In silver threads and golden hue,
It captures hearts, both old and new.

And in the dawn, as day breaks free,
The woven dreams still call to me.
For in each loop, a promise stays,
A guide through all of life's maze.

Unraveling the Mysteries Above

Gaze at the sky, a woven field,
Secrets of stars, patiently sealed.
In cosmic threads, the stories lie,
Unraveling whispers from on high.

Every shimmer, a tale unfolds,
Old as time, in stardust told.
The patterns dance, a cosmic flow,
In every twinkle, mysteries grow.

As comets streak through velvet night,
They stitch the shadows with pure light.
Galaxies swirl in wondrous grace,
A harmony forged in endless space.

With every blink, we ask and yearn,
For the secrets the heavens learn.
An infinite quest, a tireless flight,
Embracing the unknown with delight.

From constellations to nebulas bright,
The sky reveals its magic bite.
In cosmic threads, our hearts ignite,
As we unveil the mysteries bright.

Spools of Starlight and Story

In darkened skies, spools of light,
Spin tales of wonder, pure and bright.
With every whisper, a story flows,
Of distant lands where magic grows.

Each spool contains a world anew,
Of sprawling dreams and skies so blue.
We tug at threads, unravel fate,
Discovering paths that captivate.

The stars, like gems, in night's embrace,
Inviting souls to join the race.
With shimmering tales, they weave delight,
A fabric stitched of starlit night.

Every spool holds a truth so dear,
A calling that we all can hear.
In woven stories, hearts align,
Connecting souls through space and time.

As dawn approaches, dreams take flight,
Spools of starlight dance with might.
In cosmic tales we find our way,
Guided by stars till the break of day.

Enchanted Threads in the Moonlight

In twilight's soft embrace we weave,
Threads of silver, dreams conceive.
A shimmer dances, soft and light,
Whispers echo through the night.

The stars above, they twinkle bright,
Guiding our hearts with their gentle light.
Each stitch a secret, woven tight,
In the tapestry of magic's sight.

With every loop, hope takes its flight,
Embracing shadows, banishing fright.
The full moon sighs with ancient grace,
Casting blessings on this sacred space.

Through enchanted woods, we wander free,
Bound by the threads of mystery.
A world alive with unseen charms,
Leading us gently into its arms.

So let us dance beneath the glow,
As moonlight whispers, secrets flow.
In the silence where dreams take flight,
We find our magic in the night.

Whispers of Spells in the Night

Under the moon, where shadows play,
Whispers of spells drift far away.
With flickering candles, we conjure fate,
In the stillness, we cultivate.

Each rhyme we chant, a soft refrain,
Threads of magic in the night remain.
Echoes of potions on the breeze,
Awakening wonders, setting hearts at ease.

In circular dances, we align,
Binding our spirits with strands divine.
Mystical symbols glow and gleam,
As we lose ourselves in a dream.

Wands lifted high, we feel the stir,
Of ancient magic, gentle purr.
With every breath, enchantments sway,
Guiding our thoughts to light the way.

So let the night wrap us in its sigh,
As we cast our spells, reaching for the sky.
With every whisper, our dreams ignite,
In this sacred moment, all feels right.

Celestial Tangles of Fate

Beneath a canopy of stars so bright,
We find ourselves in the still of the night.
Celestial tangles weave our dreams,
Unraveling truths, or so it seems.

With every heartbeat, destinies dance,
In this cosmic web, we take a chance.
Threads of time in colors entwined,
Revealing secrets that we must find.

The moon takes heed, a watchful guide,
Casting light on paths where shadows bide.
In whispers soft, the cosmos sings,
Of ancient wisdom and the hope it brings.

Through narrow paths and twisted lanes,
We trace the lines where fate remains.
In the tapestry of sky and earth,
We discover love, and measure its worth.

So let us wander, hand in hand,
Across the stars, a sprawling land.
In these celestial tangles, we see our fate,
Entwined forever, never too late.

Shadowed Chants Beneath the Stars

In the depths of night, shadows dwell,
Chanting softly, weaving a spell.
Beneath the stars, a mystic trance,
Luring the brave to join the dance.

With whispered secrets on the breeze,
Voices rise among the trees.
Each note a promise, rich and deep,
Inviting souls from their slumber's sleep.

The moonlight's glow reveals our path,
A journey sparked by ancient wrath.
Every step unveils the unknown,
In shadowed corners, truth is sown.

So gather close, and heed the call,
As shadows rise and darkness falls.
In this communion, we shall find,
The magic lies in hearts unconfined.

As the night deepens, chant anew,
Embrace the mystery that surrounds you.
For in these shadows, within our sights,
Lie the whispers of enchanted nights.

Tapestry of Fables and Folklore

In whispered woods where shadows dance,
The stories weave a secret glance.
Of knights and dragons, tales retold,
In threads of silver and threads of gold.

Each corner holds a truth in time,
A crone's soft laugh, a child's sweet chime.
With every stitch, the past will bloom,
While ancient magic fills the room.

Here mermaids sing beneath the waves,
And gentle giants guard their caves.
In fables spun with care and craft,
Our hearts are lifted, our spirits daft.

A tapestry of dreams takes flight,
With every color shining bright.
Through every tale, our minds set free,
In woven wonders, we believe.

So gather round, dear friends of old,
And share the stories yet untold.
For in this dance of thread and lore,
The magic lives forevermore.

Dancing Lights on the Weaver's Frame

Beneath the stars, the weaver spins,
A symphony of light begins.
With every thread a story starts,
Embroidered dreams and beating hearts.

The loom awakes with gentle sighs,
As colors twirl and laughter flies.
A shimmer here, a glimmer there,
The fabric sings with joy and flair.

In twilight's glow, they rise and sway,
These dancing lights, they lead the way.
With every turn, the magic glows,
Transforming night with vibrant shows.

Through weft and warp, the tales unfold,
Of brave young minds and heroes bold.
Each woven stitch a spark divine,
In dreams of wonder, all align.

And as dawn breaks, the colors fade,
Yet whispers linger, never jade.
For what is lost in morning's light,
Is found again in hearts at night.

The Sorcery of Yarn in the Moon's Glow

In midnight's hush, the yarn entwines,
With secrets spun in shadowed signs.
A whisper of magic soft and low,
The sorcery of yarn begins to flow.

Threads of silver, threads of dreams,
In moonlit glow, enchantment beams.
Each loop, a promise, each knot, a spell,
In quiet realms where silence fell.

Mystical hands weave tales anew,
Of ancient realms and skies so blue.
The yarn, a pathway to the unknown,
In every fiber, a seed is sown.

Through cosmic dances, destiny leads,
As stars align and heartache bleeds.
A tapestry of fate unspooled,
In threads of magic, life is ruled.

So let the yarn and moonlight blend,
A sorcery that shall not end.
With every stitch, the world ignites,
In woven dreams of endless nights.

Shimmering Paths in the Night Yarn

In shadows deep where whispers weave,
A tapestry of dreams we dare believe.
With starlit threads that softly gleam,
We wander paths of midnight's dream.

Each step we take, a story spun,
Beneath the watchful, gleaming sun.
Through hidden realms where secrets sing,
We dance upon the threads of spring.

With every breath, the night awakes,
As gentle winds elude the stakes.
In vibrant hues, our hearts do blend,
A journey's path that has no end.

Through forests dark, where starlight glows,
The shimmering path of magic flows.
Past silver streams and ancient trees,
We feel the night's soft, whispering breeze.

So let us tread where shadows play,
In sparkling hues of night and day.
Along these paths, our spirits soar,
In the night's embrace, forevermore.

Cosmic Alignments in Fabric Form

Threads of fate in colors bright,
Stitching stars in radiant light.
Across the fabric of the skies,
The universe within us lies.

With every stitch, alignment found,
Celestial patterns all around.
In every fold, a tale concealed,
Of cosmic wonders, truth revealed.

Galaxies weave through mystical realms,
As ancient voices guide the helms.
From distant shores, they cast their spell,
In every heartbeat, magic swells.

A patchwork quilt of dreams untold,
In colors rich, both brave and bold.
Each corner holds a secret arc,
Of cosmic whispers, hope's bright spark.

So wander through this woven night,
Where every moment feels so right.
In fabric soft, the stars align,
As constellations brightly shine.

Enchantments Spun in Twilight's Hold

In twilight's glow, the magic breathes,
As whispered spells dance on the leaves.
With every flicker of the light,
Enchantments spun through day and night.

The stars awake, their secrets shared,
In shadows deep, our hopes are bared.
A silken thread of fate unspooled,
In twilight's grasp, our hearts have ruled.

Through whispered winds of ancient lore,
We find the keys to each locked door.
With every heartbeat, magic swells,
In twilight's hold, enchantment dwells.

In luminescent hues, we dream,
While silver streams of starlight gleam.
The twilight weaves its secrets tight,
In every corner, pure delight.

So let our spirits take their flight,
On wings of dusk, through endless night.
With each enchantment, worlds unfold,
In twilight's arms, forever bold.

The Tapestry of Shifting Winds

In winds that whisper, tales arise,
A tapestry that reaches skies.
With every breath of changing air,
We feel the magic linger there.

The colors shift, from gold to gray,
As time unfolds in dance and play.
A woven song of hope and fear,
Is carried on the breezes near.

Through valleys deep and mountains high,
The winds compose a heartfelt sigh.
In every gust, a tale reborn,
Of dreams that shimmer with the dawn.

We ride the currents, wild and free,
As the shifting tapestry we see.
Each thread a moment, bold and bright,
In nature's weave, a pure delight.

So let the winds carry us away,
On shifting paths where shadows play.
In the tapestry, our souls align,
Forever stitched in love divine.

Spectral Patterns on a Silken Loom

In twilight realms where shadows creep,
Threads of silver silently seep.
Weaving whispers, soft and true,
Spectral patterns, old and new.

Through the fabric, dreams do glide,
A tapestry with secrets wide.
Each stitch a story, rich and deep,
Guarded close, in silence, keep.

From colors bright to shadows pale,
Woven destinies softly sail.
With every touch, the echoes bloom,
Spectral patterns on a silken loom.

In moonlit hours, the threads entwine,
Bound by magic, yours and mine.
A glimpse of fables, whispers caught,
In every thread, a tale is wrought.

So linger here, where dreams reside,
Within the loom, we turn the tide.
With spectral patterns, woven art,
In the heart of night, we'll never part.

Fables in the Fabric of Dreams

In dusky realms where wishes weave,
Fables twinkle, softly leave.
Through starlit seams and moonlit grains,
A tale unfolds, as laughter gains.

From whispered winds to gentle sighs,
Dreams emerge with soft replies.
In hidden colors, stories gleam,
In the fabric of a dream, it seems.

Each shadow holds a secret tight,
Guiding hearts through velvet nights.
In every fold, adventure waits,
Fables draw us through the gates.

With every stitch, a world anew,
In threads of gold, our hopes ensue.
In tangled yarns, we laugh and cry,
Dancing fables that never die.

So take my hand, let's drift away,
In woven dreams where children play.
Through the fabric, bold and bright,
Fables whispered in the night.

Harmonies in the Dance of Shadows

When twilight calls and shadows sway,
Harmonies softly weave the gray.
In silken night, a melody,
The dance of shadows, wild and free.

Each flicker's grace, a hidden tune,
Guiding hearts 'neath the silver moon.
With every turn, the darkness sighs,
In harmony, the silence flies.

Seductive waltz of night and light,
In the silence, echoes bright.
An orchestra of dusk and dawn,
Through whispered dreams, we dance till morn.

With every step, a secret shared,
In shadowed corners, hearts laid bare.
In twilight's arms, we find our way,
With harmonies in shadows' play.

So twirl with me, through dusk's embrace,
In the silence, find our place.
With echoes sweet, we'll float and glide,
In the dance of shadows, side by side.

Celestial Crafts in the Midnight Glow

In midnight's hush, where stars emerge,
Celestial crafts begin to surge.
With every spark, a story writes,
In the glow of quiet nights.

Through cosmic threads, our tales are spun,
Mapping journeys, lost but won.
In constellations, destinies flow,
Crafted whispers in the midnight glow.

By shimmering light and gentle breeze,
We capture dreams with effortless ease.
Soaring high through endless skies,
With love and wonder in our eyes.

With every stitch, the heavens gleam,
In the tapestry of a shared dream.
Bound by stardust, hearts aglow,
In celestial crafts, we find our flow.

From dusk till dawn, let spirits soar,
As midnight's crafts unlock each door.
Together we weave, forever we'll go,
In celestial crafts of the midnight glow.

Spinning Dreams in the Twilight

In the hush of evening's glow,
Where shadows dance and secrets flow,
We weave our hopes in velvet night,
Spinning dreams in soft twilight.

Stars whisper tales on silken beams,
Guiding us through our silent dreams,
A tapestry of wishes bright,
Embraced by warmth, kissed by light.

Moonbeams spiral, casting spells,
As magic drifts from hidden wells,
Each heartbeat quickens, takes its flight,
In the cradle of the twilight.

Echoes linger in the breeze,
Caressing thoughts like gentle leaves,
With every sigh, the world feels right,
As we spin dreams in the twilight.

Nights unfurl with whispers sweet,
As we dance to the night's own beat,
In this realm where stars ignite,
We find our peace in fading light.

Enigmas Stitched with Silver Light

Beneath the moon, a silver thread,
We find the path where fate has led,
Enigmas twinkle, secrets flow,
In whispers soft, where shadows grow.

A tapestry of night unfolds,
With stories wrapped in dreams untold,
Every glimmer hides delight,
Stitched together with silver light.

We tread on paths of gleaming stone,
Where ancient spirits weave alone,
Mysteries dance in gentle height,
Calling us with their silver light.

In every glint, a promise gleams,
An echo of our childhood dreams,
With every heartbeat, hearts take flight,
Bound forever in silver light.

Lost in wonder, wrapped in song,
We wander where the brave belong,
In the twilight, bold in spite,
We unveil enigmas of silver light.

Celestial Strands of Fate

In the silence where the cosmos breathes,
We gather light from astral weaves,
Threads of fate dance in the sky,
Celestial strands that whisper why.

Galaxies twirl in gentle grace,
Each spark a story, a time, a place,
We reach for wonders, big and shy,
Writing our tales as stars pass by.

The firmament sings of dreams once sown,
In every twinkle, seeds are grown,
As we paint with cosmic light,
Tracing our paths in the velvety night.

With every breath, the universe spins,
Binding our lives with invisible sins,
Each moment captured, pure and spry,
In the dance of celestial strands that fly.

So let us weave with tender care,
Our destinies mingled in the air,
For in this vast expanse, we try,
To understand the strands of fate, oh my.

Threads of Twilight's Embrace

In twilight's gentle, soft embrace,
We find our rhythm, our sacred place,
Threads of dusk entwine and fold,
With every breath, a dream unfolds.

The horizon blushes, shades of gray,
As night creeps in to steal the day,
With whispered secrets, low and faint,
We gather wishes, young yet quaint.

Stars awaken, peeking shy,
Painting stories across the sky,
Each glimmer holds a whispered trace,
As we hold tight to twilight's grace.

With tender hearts, we weave our fate,
Under the watch of the evening state,
In every twilit, soft embrace,
We find our stories, a cherished space.

So let the night wrap us in song,
As we journey forth, where we belong,
In this sacred dance, we face,
The beauty born in twilight's embrace.

Ethereal Weavings of Time and Space

In shadowed halls where whispers play,
The threads of time like silver sway.
Each moment spun with careful thread,
A tapestry where dreams are bred.

With colors bright, the stars align,
In cosmic dance, their fates entwine.
The fabric of the night unfolds,
As secrets bloom in stories told.

Where echoes of the past reside,
And future's hopes in silence bide.
The weavers toil with nimble hands,
Creating worlds where magic stands.

A shimmer glows on twilight's edge,
On destiny's unbroken pledge.
Each tale we spin, a thread of fate,
In weavings made of love and hate.

So venture forth, let hearts embrace,
The ethereal dance of time and space.
For in this loom of night and day,
Our spirits soar where dreams hold sway.

Magical Looms of Twilight Whispers

In twilight hues where shadows sigh,
The magical looms weave tales awry.
With gentle hands, the moon does guide,
The whispers of the night collide.

From threads of dusk, the stories spill,
Of fancied realms and hidden thrill.
Each heartbeat threads the dark's embrace,
A wondrous waltz in velvet space.

Through golden rays and silken strands,
The secrets of the night expands.
In every weave, a wish concealed,
Where dreams and hopes are gently healed.

The stars, like beads, in patterns glow,
As fading light begins to slow.
We gather close, the tales refine,
In looms of twilight, all align.

So take your place, let magic flow,
In whispered threads, our spirits grow.
This tapestry, a world apart,
Unfolds the dreams that fill the heart.

The Spell of Colorful Tangles

With vibrant hues, the spell is cast,
In tangled threads, our shadows pass.
Each shimmer bright, a stroke of fate,
In colors bold, we navigate.

The playful knots, a dance so wild,
In every twist, the heart's beguiled.
A rainbow's arc, a fable spun,
In luminous bands, we come undone.

From threads of gold to deepest blue,
These vibrant strands weave dreams anew.
Each crimson strand holds passion's blaze,
In colorful tangles, we lose our ways.

So gather round, let laughter soar,
As vibrant tales unlock the door.
In every hue, a spell we weave,
In tangled magic, we believe.

So spin your dreams, let colors blend,
In spells of tangles that never end.
With every thread in hand, we find,
A world of wonder, unconfined.

Threads of Lore and Legends

Upon the loom of ancient tales,
The threads of lore weave mystic veils.
A whisper soft, a legend's wake,
In every stitch, the dreams we stake.

As moonlight bathes the silent night,
The legends rise in gentle flight.
With every knot, a memory formed,
In woven silence, magic's warmed.

Each fable spun in gold and white,
Invokes the power of lost delight.
Through every tale, our hearts partake,
In threads remembered for hope's sake.

So lift your voice, let stories sing,
Of ancient heroes and the spring.
In weaving thus, the world aligns,
As threads of lore create new signs.

Together we will stitch and share,
Our legends rich, beyond compare.
In every loop, our spirits dance,
In threads of lore, let's find our chance.

Threads of the Arcane Woven Deep

In shadows where the secrets lie,
The whispers of the ancients sigh.
A pull of fate, a woven seam,
In tangled dreams, reality's gleam.

Through emerald woods, the spirits call,
Each thread a story, binding all.
The magic swirls in soft embrace,
A dance of time, a hidden place.

With every stitch, a world unfolds,
In quiet hearts, the truth is bold.
A tapestry of hopes and fears,
Embodied tales that span the years.

As moonlight bathes the midnight sky,
The threads entwine, they never die.
In arcane knots, the past will seep,
And dreams, like starlight, softly leap.

Tangles of the Lost and Found

In alleys where the echoes hide,
The lost souls wander, side by side.
A shimmer beckons 'neath the grime,
Together weaving threads of time.

With every footstep, stories weave,
The joy and sadness they conceive.
In tangled paths, they find their way,
Through shadowed night to break of day.

Each heart a compass, searching still,
For meaning, purpose, dreams to fill.
In dusk's embrace, hope glimmers bright,
In tangled chaos, find the light.

The lost become the found once more,
Through every crack, through every door.
In bonds unbroken, strength is sown,
In every heart, a home is grown.

Folklore Stitched in Colorful Hues

In pages worn, the tales reside,
Of heroes bold and dreams untied.
With colors bright, each story sings,
Of distant lands and ancient kings.

The folklore dances on the breeze,
In laughter ringing through the trees.
A patchwork quilt of voice and lore,
Unites the heart forevermore.

With every thread, a heartbeat flows,
Of mysteries and whispered prose.
Each vibrant hue, a memory kept,
A legacy that's deeply wept.

From valleys low to mountains high,
The tales of yore will never die.
In every child, the stories bloom,
Like flowers bursting from the gloom.

Luminous Whirlwinds of Lore

In swirling winds, the voices soar,
With secrets whispered on the shore.
A tapestry of light unfolds,
In luminous tales of the bold.

The legends twirl in bright array,
While shadows linger, fade away.
Each echo brightens, fires ignite,
As lore transforms the darkest night.

With every spin, a story glows,
Of battles fought and dreams that rose.
In every heart, the sparks create,
Awakening the hand of fate.

Through cosmic winds, their spirits play,
In dance of stars, they find their way.
The whirlwind sings its vibrant tune,
Enlightening the sun and moon.

Woven Dreams of Arcane Dance

In the moonlit glade, whispers sing,
Threads of magic, in shadows they cling.
Dancing lights twirl, a celestial race,
Weaved in the air, tales of time and space.

Leaves flutter softly, a sacred refrain,
Echoes of laughter, joy intertwined with pain.
Spirits in silence, glimmering bright,
Wrapped in the fabric of the starry night.

A tapestry spun, with dusk as the loom,
Crafting the dreams that in twilight bloom.
Each knot a secret, each thread a sigh,
Woven desires that soar and fly.

As the dawn breaks, colors unfurl,
A crown of splendor, the day starts to whirl.
Yet in the whispers of the soft summer breeze,
Live the arcane dances of the ancient trees.

So linger a moment, let the world slow,
In woven dreams where the lost pathways flow.
Surrender your heart, let the magic enhance,
And lose yourself deep in the arcane dance.

Mystical Hues in the Twilight

As daylight fades to gentle hues,
The sky blinks softly, casting clues.
Mystical shades in lavender flow,
Whispers of secrets, twilight aglow.

Crickets begin their serenade sweet,
As shadows awaken on paths where we meet.
Stars peer shyly through curtains of gray,
Guiding lost wanderers who drift their way.

The air holds magic, thick as perfume,
Painted with dreams that in silence loom.
Echoes of laughter in the dusk's embrace,
Wrap around hearts in this sacred space.

A canvas stretched wide, the night softly calls,
With stories of wonders that linger in halls.
Under the gaze of a crescent moon's light,
Hearts intertwine in the spell of the night.

So dance in the twilight, let worries depart,
Embrace the mysteries, with an open heart.
For in these moments, with magic in sight,
Life's finest colors emerge in the night.

Secrets in the Tapestry of Time

Time flows like rivers, with whispers of old,
Each turn a story, waiting to be told.
In the fabric of moments, threads interlace,
Holding the secrets of time and of space.

Wisps of remembrance float down the years,
Stitched in the laughter, woven with tears.
Echoes dance lightly on the edges of dreams,
Binding the past to the world as it seems.

In moonbeams streaming through elderwood trees,
Lie tales of enchantment carried by the breeze.
With every heartbeat, the past comes alive,
In the tapestry's weave, forgotten hopes thrive.

Listen closely; the whispers they bring,
Tales of the lost and the wonders of spring.
Each wrinkle a journey, where stories entwine,
In the delicate threads of fate's grand design.

So delve into ages, where mysteries arc,
Seek out the light in the depth of the dark.
For in every moment, both tender and prime,
Lies the heartbeat of life, in the tapestry of time.

Fantasia of Threads and Shadows

In realms of fantasy, where dreams intertwine,
Shadows and threads weave a tale so divine.
Colors dance wildly, swirling and bright,
With each whispered secret, igniting the night.

Winds sing through branches, a magical tune,
Weaving together the earth and the moon.
Spirits of dusk guide the colors of fate,
Crafting with echoes, so intricate, so late.

With threads of the sun, and shadows of dreams,
Life flows like water in crystalline streams.
Every fold and twist, a story unseen,
In the canvas of night, where wonders convene.

Fantasia whispers, inviting the brave,
To dance in the twilight, in shadows they wave.
Hold fast to the magic, embrace the unknown,
For in this illusion, true beauty is shown.

So take up the challenge, this journey of cheer,
To weave with the shadow, and dance without fear.
For life is but threads, a fantasmic parade,
Entwined in the shadows, true dreams are made.

Secrets Woven in the Fog

In the hush of twilight's breath,
Shadows dance with ancient trees,
Whispers weave through misty depths,
Carrying tales on the evening breeze.

Silhouettes of secrets hide,
Among the blooms that softly sigh,
Glimmers of light in fleeting flight,
Echoes of what once was nigh.

A silver thread that binds the night,
Through hidden paths where dreams align,
Each strand a story, a heart so bright,
Carved in the fog, almost divine.

Listen closely, hearts can hear,
The laughter lost in time's embrace,
As the stars above draw near,
To weave their light in twilight's space.

For in these veils of misty grace,
Lies the magic of what we seek,
A tapestry of time and place,
Secrets woven, soft yet sleek.

Enchanted Fibers of the Night

Under the cloak of indigo skies,
Silken threads of raven hue,
Dance and twirl as magic flies,
Weaving dreams that feel so true.

Glowing embers from stars descend,
Embraced by winds that gently sigh,
Whispering tales without end,
In the twilight where spirits lie.

With each shimmer, a longing stirs,
A tapestry stitched with light,
Through the dark, the midnight purrs,
Binding souls in restful night.

Glistening like dew on the ground,
Every fiber a wish unfurled,
In enchanted patterns, hope is found,
Bringing magic to the world.

So hold these threads close to your heart,
For they carry dreams from afar,
In the silence, let them impart,
The wonders spun beneath each star.

Mystical Patterns in the Sky

Above the world where wishes drift,
Patterns paint the velvet black,
Cosmic tapestries that lovingly lift,
The dreams of travelers who seek to track.

With every sparkle, a story told,
Celestial dances drawing near,
In the night, the universe bold,
Arraying its wonders, crystal clear.

Shooting stars weave through the expanse,
Fleeting moments of sheer delight,
In the silence, the heart finds chance,
To grasp the threads of hope and light.

The moon a muse, soft and bright,
Guides the wanderers on their way,
Glimmers and shadows, side by side,
In the mystical patterns where dreams sway.

So look above and let it soar,
Each twinkling gem a beckoning sign,
In the firmament's embrace, explore,
The endless life in the divine.

The Weaving of Forgotten Dreams

In the fabric of the old and gray,
Forgotten dreams begin to glow,
Threads of gold in disarray,
Holding memories from long ago.

Stitched with hope, then delicately torn,
These whispers linger on the breeze,
Once bright visions, now forlorn,
Seeking solace among the trees.

Yet in the night, they dare to rise,
Embraced by shadows, held so tight,
Voices echoing through the skies,
Rekindling dreams lost to the light.

Transforming stories, lost and found,
In a heartbeat, they reappear,
In quiet corners, softly bound,
The weaving whispers, "We are here."

So fear not the dreams that fade away,
For in the twilight, there's a seam,
Where all forgotten hopes shall play,
The artful weaving of every dream.

Chronicles of the Enchanted Fabric

In the loom of fate, threads intertwine,
Whispers of magic in each design.
The weaver's hands dance with ancient lore,
Spinning tales of light forevermore.

Colors of destiny, woven with grace,
Patterns of dreams, in this sacred place.
Each stitch a secret, each knot a sign,
Binding together the worlds that align.

A tapestry blooms in the softest light,
Guarding the stories hidden from sight.
With every pull of the shimmering string,
Echoes of time in the fabric sing.

Threads from the stars, with silver and gold,
Mapping the journeys of the brave and bold.
In the weave of the night, the mysteries lay,
Unraveled by dawn's gentle ray.

Mysteries Wrought in Colorful Threads

A tapestry hangs in the heart of the night,
Colors that shimmer, a dazzling sight.
Threads of the rainbow, woven with care,
Carrying secrets of dreams meant to share.

Each hue a story, each swirl a spell,
Whispers of wonder, in silence they dwell.
Beneath the moon's gaze, the patterns sway,
Enchanting the souls who wander this way.

Silken intentions, a fabric of fate,
Woven with purpose, too wondrous to sate.
From crimson desires to tranquil blue,
Mysteries linger in every hue.

As daylight breaks through the canvas of night,
The threads reveal tales bathed in soft light.
In colors alive, their whispers persist,
The stories of past and future entwist.

Fantasies Interlaced with Night

In shadows woven, where dreams take flight,
Fantasies blossom under the starlit night.
Stitch by stitch, the cosmos unfolds,
With shimmering wonders and tales yet untold.

Moonbeams are gathered, entwined with the dark,
In a quilt of enchantment, each patch leaves a mark.
The fabric of night, with threads of the day,
Interlaced in a harmony, cosmic ballet.

Stars wink in laughter, as stories ignite,
The threads that connect us twinkle so bright.
Woven with wishes, our hearts start to gleam,
In the dreams that we chase, we find our true theme.

From dusk until dawn, the fabric does gleam,
Carrying whispers of every lost dream.
In this realm of twilight, we find our way back,
To the threads of our lives, in silver and black.

Secrets of the Cosmic Spindle

In the quiet of night, the spindle does hum,
Spinning the secrets, where wonders come from.
Threads of the cosmos, in twilight they gleam,
Whispers of magic, like the softest dream.

Each twirl reveals glimpses, of realms far away,
Where stars weave connections, in night's grand ballet.
Fates intertwining in shimmering threads,
Guiding the lost through the paths that it spreads.

In the heart of the fabric, a truth softly lies,
Echoes of love beneath the vast skies.
Secrets entangled in fibers of light,
Binding the universe, day into night.

As the spindle spins on, the stories entwine,
A dance of creation, both subtle and fine.
Through the tapestry woven, we find our own thread,
In the secrets of night, the magic is spread.

Starlit Tangles and Spells

In the still of the night, secrets bloom,
Whispers of magic drift from the loom.
Fingers entwined with threads of the past,
Starlit tangles where dreams are cast.

A glimmering path through shadows crept,
In the heart of the woods, where silence wept.
Each spell woven tight with intentions bold,
Stories of wonder and daring unfold.

By the light of the moon, the enchantments play,
Illuminating the night, keeping darkness at bay.
Beneath the vast sky, hearts softly swell,
In starlit tangles, we weave our spell.

With laughter and love, we gather our might,
Harnessing visions that dance in the light.
The tapestry glows, as the magic ignites,
In a world made of starlight, we claim our rights.

So come, take my hand, let the fantasy soar,
Through starlit tangles, we'll wander and explore.
Beneath all the stars, our spirits will meld,
In the embrace of the night, our dreams are upheld.

Chronicles of the Sorceress' Thread

In shadows and light, the sorceress weaves,
Such intricacies born from her heart's leaves.
With wisdom of ages, her fingers glide,
Through tales of the ancients, where secrets abide.

The thread of the cosmos, so delicate spun,
Ancient stories emerge as she's begun.
Choices and fates, knotting tight with each twist,
In the chronicles held by a magical mist.

Her lantern aglow in the depths of the night,
Illuminating pathways both wild and bright.
Her voice echoes softly, a melody rare,
Guiding lost wanderers through darkened despair.

As patterns unfold, the stars seem to sing,
A ballad of magic, of hope that they bring.
With every new stitch, a spell unconfined,
In the chronicles binding all of mankind.

So lift up your hearts and listen, believe,
To the tales of the thread, all souls interleave.
In sorceress whispers, let futures be bred,
For the magic lies deep in the weavings we thread.

Moonlit Labyrinths of Color

In a labyrinth deep where the moonlight spills,
Colors burst forth with enchanting thrills.
Winding pathways of sapphire and gold,
Secrets unfurl in the stories untold.

Through shadows and starlight, the journey unfolds,
Each twist and each turn, a new tale it molds.
Petals of crimson, the fragrance so sweet,
In moonlit adventures, our spirits shall meet.

The dance of the night, a magical trance,
A symphony singing, enchanting romance.
With laughter and wonder, we step so light,
Through the labyrinth bright under pale silver light.

With echoes of laughter, the colors swirl high,
A kaleidoscope gleaming beneath the vast sky.
Every corner and crest, a treasure to give,
In moonlit mazes, our dreams come alive.

So wander with me where the wonders abound,
In moonlit labyrinths, our joy shall be found.
With hearts all aglow, let our spirits take flight,
In vibrant adventures, we'll dance with the night.

Tapestry of the Celestial Dance

In the vast stretch of night, where stars do align,
A tapestry woven with patterns divine.
The cosmos entwined in a graceful embrace,
In the celestial dance, we find our place.

With whispers of starlight, the comets all glide,
Through dreams and through wishes, side by side.
Each thread tells a story, each knot has a rhyme,
Painting the heavens in rhythm and time.

As planets spin softly, in perfect accord,
The music of spheres an enchanting reward.
Caught in the wonder, we sway with the moon,
In the tapestry's heart, we'll never feel gloom.

So journey with me through the stellar expanse,
Where magic abounds in the cosmic romance.
With every new dawn, our spirits enhance,
In the tapestry woven of a celestial dance.

Embrace the enchantment, let worries dissolve,
In the light of the stars, our dreams shall evolve.
For in this grand weave of fate and of chance,
We'll find higher realms in the celestial dance.

Spun Sorrows Beneath Mystic Skies

Amidst the shadows, dreams are spun,
With whispers of moonlight, a tale begun.
Each teardrop falls, a shimmer bright,
Beneath the mystic skies of night.

Winds carry secrets, ancient and deep,
Through the forest where lost spirits weep.
In silence they dance, a sorrowful waltz,
Binding the hearts of those who halt.

Through tangled branches, the echoes soar,
Of laughter and grief, forevermore.
In every heartbeat, they weave and bind,
Spun sorrows whisper, a truth confined.

Yet hope ignites in the darkest space,
As stars awaken in their brilliant grace.
For every shadow holds light within,
A tapestry woven, where dreams begin.

So wander the paths where magic thrives,
And find the joy in all that survives.
Beneath those skies, let your spirit fly,
Embrace the sorrows, let your heart sigh.

Riddles in a Cloak of Night

Hidden in darkness, the riddles arise,
Cloaked in whispers beneath starlit skies.
They dance on the breeze, eluding our grasp,
In the silence of night, they twist and clasp.

Echoes of laughter, a flicker of hope,
Through shadows they linger, like shadows we mope.
Each answer, a treasure to seek and to find,
In the depths of the night, where secrets unwind.

The moon drips silver, a guide overhead,
As old tales are spun of the lost and the dead.
With every heartbeat, a question takes flight,
A tapestry woven in riddles of night.

Through misty adventures, our spirits are shown,
The paths that we wander, the seeds we have sown.
For knowledge is power, wrapped in delight,
In the cloak of the night, where mysteries write.

And as dawn approaches, the riddles may fade,
Yet the echoes and whispers will never evade.
For once they are spoken, forever they gleam,
Riddles in darkness, a heart's treasured dream.

Threads of Glory

In the loom of existence, threads intertwine,
Each moment a stitch, in a grand design.
From shadows of doubt, to beams of light,
The fabric of life weaves bold and bright.

A tapestry rich with colors and dreams,
Of laughter and heartache, of wild, daring schemes.
With every small triumph, a new thread we clasp,
Embroidering hopes in a radiant grasp.

Between joy and sorrow, the fibers align,
Creating a pattern uniquely divine.
Through each twist and turn, the journey unfolds,
Threads of glory, the story then molds.

As life's needle dances, we learn and we grow,
Each stitch a reminder of all that we know.
In the tapestry woven, our hearts will reside,
Threads of glory, with us as our guide.

So cherish the moments, both small and grand,
For they shape our journey, their purpose at hand.
As the loom keeps on turning, may your spirit soar high,
In the threads of glory, let your dreams fly.

Paths Unknown

Upon the horizon, where twilight meets dawn,
Lie paths untraveled, where few have gone.
With courage as armor, the heart beats strong,
To tread on the trails where the brave belong.

Through forests of whispers and mountains so grand,
Each step is a choice, with fate close at hand.
The unknown may beckon, tempting the soul,
In the quest for the truth, we discover our role.

With every encounter, the magic unfolds,
In tales of the past, and of heroes bold.
The stars above shimmer, a map drawn in light,
Guiding the wanderer through the shrouded night.

So venture with wonder, and let your heart lead,
For paths unknown nourish the soul's deepest need.
In the journey of life, as we roam and we stray,
We find whispered treasures that light up our way.

The laughter of friends and the warmth of the sun,
Are gifts on this journey that's just begun.
Embrace the unknown, let it fill you with cheer,
In paths unexplored, find what you hold dear.

Constellations Entwined in Whispers

Beneath the vast canvas of eternal night,
Constellations whisper, their stories take flight.
In the tapestry woven of stardust and dreams,
They map out a dance, as the cosmos gleams.

With every soft shimmer, a tale is revealed,
In the hearts of the dreamers who long to be healed.
The silence of space, like a lullaby sweet,
Calls forth the souls on their journey to meet.

Entwined in the magic, where wishes shall soar,
The constellations beckon, forever explore.
For each twinkling star holds a dream to unfold,
A promise of wonders and secrets untold.

As whispers of ancients drift down from the skies,
Let the light guide your heart, let it rise and arise.
In this cosmic embrace, where possibilities bloom,
Become one with the universe, let your spirit assume.

So gaze at the heavens, let your thoughts take flight,
For constellations twine in the fabric of night.
Each star holds a wish, a flame in the dark,
As the whispers of wonders ignite every spark.

Rainbows Unraveled by Dawn

In the hush of morning's glow,
Colors whisper tales unknown,
A canvas stretched, soft and slow,
As shadows tremble, softly blown.

With dew-kissed petals glistening bright,
Nature hums a gentle tune,
Each hue unfolds in brilliant light,
Awakening beneath the moon.

Promises lie in the mist's embrace,
As sunlight breaks the velvet shroud,
Transforming tears to joy's sweet grace,
A masterpiece of beauty proud.

Fluttering wings in quiet flight,
Ballet of colors in the air,
Embers dance in a world so bright,
Held by dreams and wishes rare.

So listen close to dawn's soft sigh,
As rainbows weave through waking skies,
A tapestry where hopes can fly,
Unraveled by the light that dies.

Echoes of Enchantment in the Yarn

In twilight's hush, a story weaves,
Where threads of magic intertwine,
Each stitch, a secret heart believes,
In whispered dreams where fates align.

With silver strands of moonlit grace,
The loom spins tales of ages past,
Enchantment finds a sacred space,
In warmth that holds, forever cast.

Voices echo in the tapestry,
A chorus sung in vibrant thread,
The sorrows of eternity,
And joys that shimmer 'round the bed.

Time unfurls on a silver seam,
Each pattern whispers, soft and clear,
A woven web of every dream,
Caught in the threads of love and fear.

So let the yarn unravel slow,
Revealing mysteries intertwined,
For in each knot, the heart must show,
The magic that we hope to find.

The Dance of Colors in the Breeze

Amidst the meadows wild and free,
The colors sway with playful cheer,
They twirl and leap in harmony,
As nature's joy draws ever near.

Each blossom shares a vibrant tale,
A tapestry of scents and sights,
With gentle gusts that weave and sail,
Creating magic in the heights.

The sun ignites a canvas bright,
Where every hue finds space to play,
In every shimmer, pure delight,
As day breaks softly, chased away.

Soft whispers ride the summer winds,
While laughter echoes through the trees,
In nature's arms, the moment spins,
A dance of colors in the breeze.

So close your eyes and feel the sway,
Let vibrant dreams begin to tease,
For in the dance of light's array,
We find our hearts at perfect peace.

Spellbound Fragments of Time

In twilight's grasp, the past unfolds,
With fragments caught in amber light,
Each glittering moment gently holds,
A spellbound tale of day and night.

Time swirls like leaves upon the stream,
Caught in the weave of whispered breath,
Where echoes linger, softly gleam,
In stories spun beyond our death.

The clock's hands dance in rhythmic flow,
A heartbeat lost in dreams of yore,
In every tick, a chance to grow,
To gather moments evermore.

With shadows casting memories deep,
A tapestry of light and dark,
Each thread a promise that we keep,
In every sigh, a longing spark.

So let the magic bubble forth,
Embrace the fragments cast in time,
For in each memory's gentle worth,
We find our hearts, our souls, our rhyme.

9 781805 634720